Camping

BY M. J. YORK

Published by The Child's World®
1980 Lookout Drive • Mankato, MN 56003-1705
800-599-READ • www.childsworld.com

Acknowledgments
The Child's World®: Mary Berendes, Publishing Director
Red Line Editorial: Editorial direction
The Design Lab: Design
Amnet: Production

Photographs ©: Angela Jones/Shutterstock Images, cover (top),
1, 3; Stockbyte/Thinkstock, cover (center), 1; tkemot/Shutterstock
Images, cover (bottom), 1; PhotoDisc, back cover (top left), 6, 15;
Feng Yu/Shutterstock Images, back cover (top right), 14; Brenda
Carson/Shutterstock Images, back cover (bottom), 13; carroteater/
Shutterstock Images, back cover (bottom-left), 12; Olesia Bilkei/
Shutterstock Images, 5; Ryan McVay/Thinkstock, 7; Lightspring/
Shutterstock Images, 8; Jami Garrison/Shutterstock Images, 9;
simoly/Shutterstock Images, 10; Bikeworldtravel/Shutterstock
Images, 11; abadonian/Thinkstock, 16; bissell/Thinkstock, 17;
DigitalVision, 18–19 ; Ryan McVay/Thinkstock, 20–21

ISBN 9781626873278
LCCN 2014930661

Printed in the United States of America
Mankato, MN
July, 2014
PA02222

ABOUT THE AUTHOR

*M. J. York is a children's author
and editor who lives in Minnesota.
She has loved the outdoors her entire
life and started camping, hiking,
and canoeing at a young age.*

CONTENTS

CAMPING IN NATURE

Have you ever spent time in nature? Maybe you have seen a deer in the woods. Or maybe you have gone hiking in the mountains. Perhaps you have slept in a tent or a **camper**.

These are all things people do when they go camping. They go into nature for a day

THINGS TO DO WHILE CAMPING
- stargaze
- go hiking
- look for animal tracks or wildflowers
- toast marshmallows
- write or draw in a journal
- bird-watch
- go swimming or boating
- take pictures

or two, a week, or even for months. They live, play, eat, and sleep outside. They hear rushing water and the wind in the trees. They connect with nature.

WHAT IS CAMPING?

Camping is living and sleeping outside for a short time. Often, people sleep in tents. People go camping for fun because they enjoy nature. Campers might hike, boat, or swim. Sometimes, they see wildlife—birds, raccoons, deer, or even bears!

People have always needed to survive in the **wilderness**. They've used skills such as building a shelter, making a fire, and finding their way. People started camping for fun in the 1800s. Camping in nature was a break from city life.

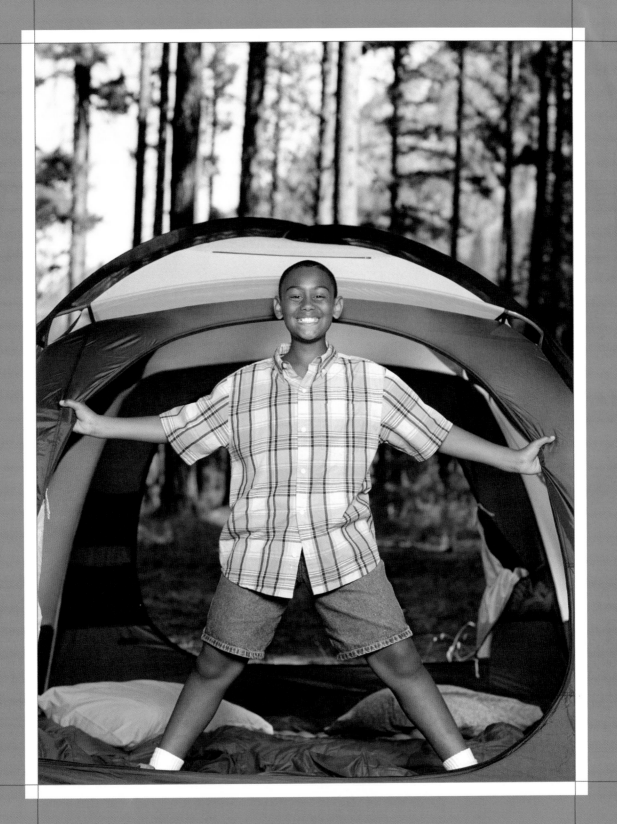

Take a break and camp in the woods!

CAMPGROUNDS

Some people drive cars into campgrounds. Some **pitch** tents in campsites. Others sleep in campers or **recreational vehicles** (RVs).

Campsites are areas where people can pitch tents or park their campers or RVs. Many campsites have picnic tables and fire pits. A campground is made up of many campsites. Campgrounds usually have water to drink. They also have bathrooms. Some have showers. Often, there is something fun to do at a campground such as going on a hike.

A picnic table is a great place to share a meal with others.

A campground might have a playground or a picnic area, too.

Campgrounds are found all over the United States. In Maine, campers can pitch tents by the ocean. In North Carolina, people can drive their campers into the mountains. Campgrounds offer something for everyone.

PARK RANGERS

Many campgrounds are in state or national parks. Governments run these parks. Most state and national parks have a ranger station. Park rangers can help if there is a problem. Sometimes, they lead hikes. They teach about the plants and animals in the park.

Park rangers help keep campgrounds safe and fun for everyone.

BACKPACKING

Some campers do not drive to their campsites. Instead, they go backpacking. They hike far into the wilderness. They carry everything they need in backpacks. Some places have walk-in campsites for backpackers. In other

Some people camp in the wilderness.

places, backpackers can pitch their tents where they like.

Backpackers go far from other people. They bring their own water or **purify** water they find. Backpackers have to bring their trash back with them. They bury their waste. This is called "leave no trace." Backpackers are careful not to **disturb** nature.

PADDLE OR RIDE
There are other ways to go camping that do not involve driving. People might paddle a canoe or a kayak to their campsites. Some ride bikes or motorcycles. Others ride horses or even bring llamas to carry their gear!

Try biking to your next campsite!

BEING PREPARED

People need to bring their own shelter and food when they camp. Many campers stay in tents. Tents protect them from the weather. They keep out bugs, too!

Campers can choose sleeping bags made for warmer or cooler weather. Many people like to use an air mattress or sleeping pad. It makes sleeping on the ground more comfortable. Some campers bring their pillows. Others rest their heads on their clothes!

People eat many fun and yummy foods

Be sure to take a sleeping bag when you go camping.

while camping. They might eat trail mix with raisins and nuts for a snack. Some campers cook on a camp stove. Others cook right over a fire. Some people even catch their own fish for dinner!

WE WANT S'MORE!
A favorite camping dessert is s'mores. Roast a marshmallow on a stick. Then, sandwich it with a chocolate square between two graham crackers. Delicious!

S'mores are a yummy camping treat!

DRESS FOR SUCCESS

It is important to dress for the weather. In cold or wet weather, campers choose clothes that keep them warm and dry. They wear layers they can take off or put on. They do not wear cotton fabric or jeans. When jeans get wet, they make you feel colder.

In hot weather, campers wear sun hats and sunscreen. They pick light-colored clothes that fit loosely. And they drink lots of water! Some people bring swimsuits so they can take a dip.

Comfortable shoes are important, especially for backpackers. Good sneakers work around the campsite and on short hikes. People who are hiking all day may choose

A good hat will help keep the sun off your face.

hiking boots. Wet socks are very uncomfortable. It is smart to bring extra pairs.

OTHER THINGS TO PACK
- A flashlight or lantern makes it bright at night.
- A pocketknife, saw, or hand ax prepares firewood.
- Matches start the fire.
- Rope can make a clothesline or help tie down the tent in bad weather.
- Pots, utensils, dishes, dish soap, and towels are needed for making meals and cleaning up.
- A first aid kit is important in case someone gets hurt.
- Remember to bring personal items like soap and toothpaste.
- Don't forget the fun! Bring along card games or books to read. Pack a ball to toss around. Bring binoculars and a camera, too!

Flashlights are handy when it's dark outside.

STAYING SAFE

Accidents can happen while people are camping. But campers who have the right gear and knowledge usually stay safe.

Fire safety is important on camping trips. It is safest to build a fire in a fire pit. Do not build a fire if it is very dry. It could

POISON IVY AND TICKS

Two common hazards in the woods are poison ivy and ticks. Watch for poison ivy and avoid it. Its leaves grow in threes and are often waxy. Poison ivy gives people a red, itchy rash. Keep ticks off with bug spray. Wear a hat and long pants tucked into socks. Stay out of tall grass and bushes. Check for ticks and remove them with tweezers.

Make sure you have an adult's help if you plan to chop wood or start a fire.

start a **wildfire**! Keep fires small and under control. It is important to put out fires completely.

Most of the time, animals will not bother campers if they do not bother the animals! But, animals are attracted to food. People who are car camping should put all their food back in the car. Backpackers should seal food in plastic and put it far from the campsite.

When hiking, it is safest to stay on marked trails. Bring a map and a **compass**. A compass helps hikers find their way. Ask an adult how to use a compass before you go hiking.

A map will help you find the most scenic locations.

It is not hard to get lost in the woods. When people get lost, search parties look for them. Campers who are lost can blow a whistle, light a smoky fire, or signal with a mirror to help rescuers find them.

CONNECTING WITH NATURE

Camping teaches people to love nature and the earth. They learn to camp carefully so they do not disturb nature. They pick up their trash. They do not pick flowers or take rocks home. Remember: Take only photos and leave only footprints.

Camping gets people out of their homes and into nature. They leave behind work and school

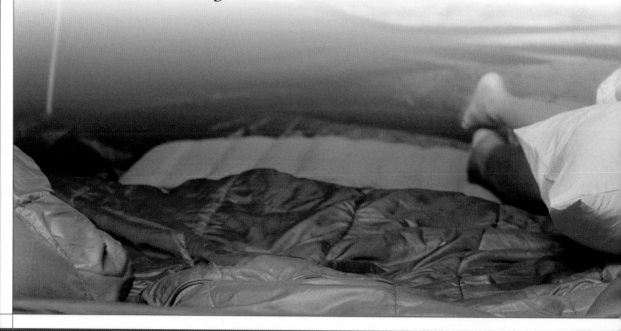

Camping is fun for everyone in your family!

and chores. They see trees and flowers and birds and wild animals. They might learn new skills, such as making a fire or identifying animal tracks. They might see natural wonders, such as mountains or waterfalls. They make fun memories that last a lifetime!

GLOSSARY

camper (KAM-pur): A camper is a motor vehicle or trailer used for sleeping and living while camping. Some people sleep in a camper instead of a tent.

compass (KUM-pus): A compass is a device that shows which way is north. People can use a map and a compass to find their way.

disturb (di-STURB): To disturb is to change or damage something. Be careful not to disturb nature.

pitch (pich): To pitch a tent is to set it up. It is hard to pitch a tent in the rain.

purify (PYUR-i-fye): To purify is to make something clean. Purify water from a lake or stream before you drink it.

recreational vehicles (REK-ree-ay-shun-ul VEE-ik-ulz): Recreational vehicles are large vehicles used for camping. Recreational vehicles often have a bed, a table, a kitchen, and even a bathroom.

wilderness (WIL-dur-nis): Wilderness is wild land where few people live or visit. Some people go backpacking in the wilderness.

wildfire (WIYLD-fi-ur): A wildfire is a fire in nature that is not controlled. A campfire can start a wildfire if it is not put out completely.

TO LEARN MORE

BOOKS

Brunelle, Lynn. *Camp Out! The Ultimate Kids' Guide from the Backyard to the Backwoods.* New York: Workman, 2007.

Great Things to Do Outside. New York: DK Children, 2014.

White, Kate. *Cooking in a Can: More Campfire Recipes for Kids.* Salt Lake City, UT: Gibbs Smith, 2006.

WEB SITES

Visit our Web site for links about camping:
childsworld.com/links

Note to Parents, Teachers, and Librarians: We routinely verify our Web links to make sure they are safe and active sites. So encourage your readers to check them out!

INDEX